ON THE ROAD AGAIN

Words and Music by
WILLIE NELSON

Verse 2:
On the road again.
Goin' places that I've never been.
Seein' things that I may never see again,
And I can't wait to get on the road again.
(To 2nd ending)

Always On My Mind

Words and Music by
WAYNE THOMPSON,
MARK JAMES and JOHNNY CHRISTOPHER

BLAME IT ON THE TIMES

Words and Music by
WILLIE NELSON

COMIN' BACK TO TEXAS

By
JULIE PAUL,
CHUCK JOYCE and KENNETH THREADGILL

Lively 2-Beat

There's a land I know ____ where the blue bon - net grows, ____ and it's par - a - dise to me. ____

strong. _____ Com - ing back to

you my dear old Tex - as,

that's where I be - long. _____

BEER BARREL POLKA
(Roll Out The Barrel)

Based on the European success "SKODA LASKY"

Words and Music by
LEW BROWN, WLADIMIR A. TIMM,
VASEK ZEMAN and JAROMIE VEJVODA

Fast Fox Trot *(like a polka)*

22

SOME OTHER TIME

Words and Music by
WILLIE NELSON

MONA LISA

By
JAY LIVINGSTON and RAY EVANS

Mo - na Li - sa, Mo - na Li - sa, men have named you. You're so

like the la - dy with the mys-tic smile. Is it on - ly 'cause you're lone-ly they have

blamed you for that Mo - na Li - sa strange-ness in your smile? Do you

smile to tempt a lov-er, ___ Mo - na Li - sa, _____ or is this your way to hide a bro - ken

heart? Man - y dreams have been brought to your door - step. They just lie there, and they

die there. Are you warm, are you real, Mo - na Li - sa, or just a

cold and lone - ly, love - ly work of art? Mo - na art?

TILL I GAIN CONTROL AGAIN

Words and Music by
RODNEY CROWELL

Slowly

1. Just like the sun o-ver the moun-tain top,_____
2. 4. *(See additional lyrics)*
3. *(Instrumental)*

mf

L.H. tacet first time

you know I'll al-ways_____ come a-

gain._____

You know I

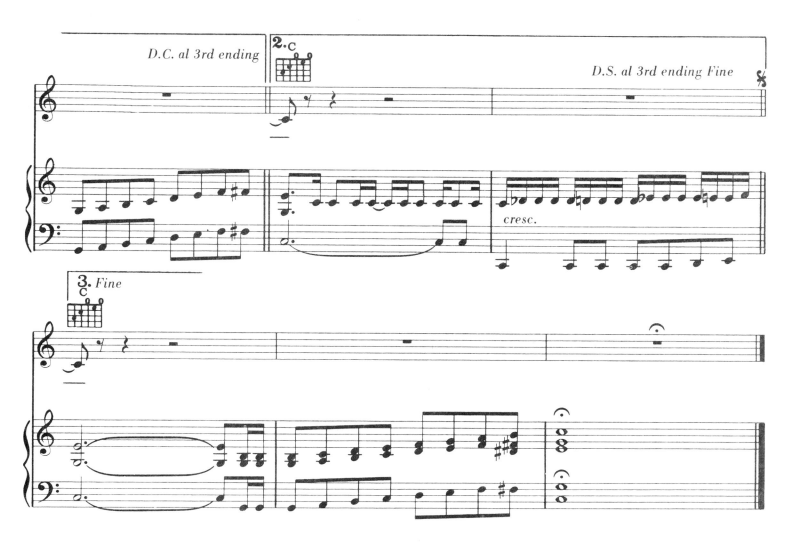

2. I have never gone so wrong as for tellin' lies to you.
   What you've seen is what I've been.
   There is nothin' that I can hide from you.
   You see me better than I can.

   To Chorus:

3. *Instrumental*

4. Just like a lighthouse, you must stand alone;
   Landmark a sailor's journey's end.
   No matter what sea I've been sailing on,
   I'll always roll this way again.

   To Chorus:

My Love For The Rose

Words and Music by
WILLIE NELSON

Moderate waltz ♩ = 92

Was it some-thing ___ I did, Lord, ___ a life-time ___ a-go? Am I

just now ___ re-pay-ing ___ a debt that ___ I

UNDO THE RIGHT

Words and Music by
WILLIE NELSON and HANK COCHRAN

HEARTACHES OF A FOOL

Words and Music by
WALT BREELAND,
PAUL BUSKIRK and WILLIE NELSON

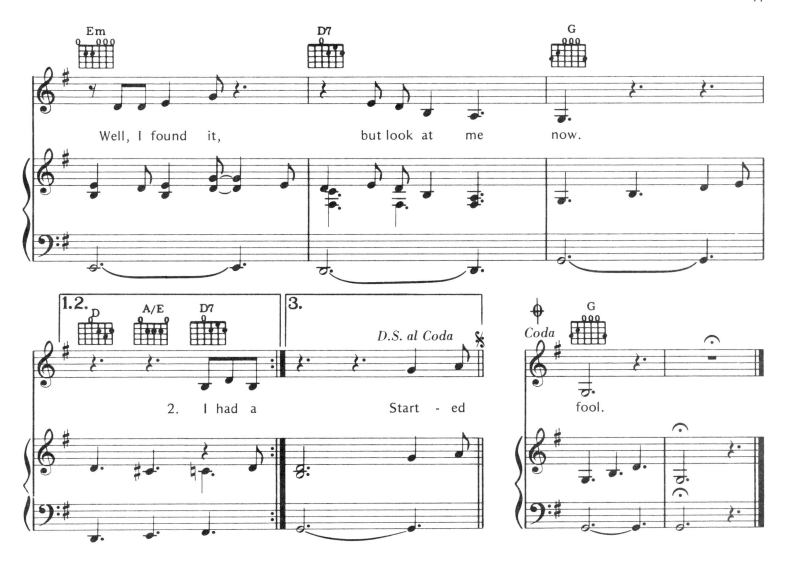

Well, I found it, but look at me now.

1.2. 2. I had a

3. D.S. al Coda Start - ed

Coda fool.

2. I had a sweetheart who would love me forever.
   Didn't need her; I would reign all alone.
   And look at me; I'm the king of a cold, lonely castle,
   And the queen of my heart is gone.

3. Gather 'round me, you fools, for a dollar.
   Listen to me, and a lesson you'll learn.
   Wealth is happiness and love,
   Sent from Heaven above,
   And the fires of ambition will burn.

FADED LOVE

Words and Music by
BOB WILLS and JOHNNY WILLS

2. As I think of the past and all the pleasure we had,
   As I watch the mating of the dove,
   And it was in the springtime that we said goodbye.
   I remember our faded love.

   (To Chorus)

GOOD TIMES

Words and Music by
WILLIE NELSON

Verse 2:
When I rolled rubber tires in the driveway,
Pulled a purse on a string across the highway;
Classify these as good times, good times.

(To Chorus:)

Verse 3:
Go to school, fight a war, working steady;
Meet a girl, fall in love, for I'm ready;
Classify these as good times, good times.

Verse 4:
Here I sit with a drink and a memory,
But I'm not cold, I'm not wet, and I'm not hungry;
Classify these as good times, good times.

I'M GONNA SIT RIGHT DOWN AND WRITE MYSELF A LETTER

Words by
JOE YOUNG

Music by
FRED E. AHLERT

CITY OF NEW ORLEANS

By
STEVE GOODMAN

Pass-in' towns___ that have___ no name___ and

freight - yards___ full of old___ black men,___ and the grave - yards ___ of the.

rust - ed au - to - mo - biles.___

1. Good morn - ing A - mer - i - ca,___ how are___ you?   Say
2. Good morn - ing A - mer - i - ca,___ how are___ you?   Said
3. Good night, A - mer - i - ca,___ how are___ you?   Said

I'll be gone____ five hun - dred miles ____ when the day ____ is done.

2. Dealin' card games with the old men in the club car,
   Penny a point ain't no one keepin' score.
   Pass the paper bag that holds the bottle;
   Feel the wheels grumblin' 'neath the floor;
   And the sons of Pullman porters, and the sons of engineers
   Ride their father's magic carpet made of steel.
   Mothers with their babes asleep are rockin' to the gentle beat
   And the rhythm of the rails is all they feel.

3. Night time on the City of New Orleans,
   Changin' cars in Memphis, Tennessee;
   Halfway home, we'll be there by mornin',
   Thru the Mississippi darkness rollin' down to the sea.
   But all the towns and people seem to fade into a bad dream,
   And the steel rail still ain't heard the news;
   The conductor sings his songs again;
   The passengers will please refrain,
   This train's got the disappearin' railroad blues.

What a Wonderful World

Words and Music by
GEORGE DAVID WEISS and BOB THIELE

PLEASE COME TO BOSTON

Words and Music by
DAVE LOGGINS

ADDITIONAL LYRICS

Verse 3.
    Please come to L.A. to live forever
    A California life alone is just too hard to build
    I live in a house that looks out over the ocean
    And there's some stars that fell from the sky
    Living up on the hill
    Please come to L.A., she just said no,
    Boy, won't you come home to me.
Repeat Chorus

TAKE IT TO THE LIMIT

Words and Music by
DON HENLEY,
GLENN FREY and RANDY MEISNER

SEVEN SPANISH ANGELS

Words and Music by
EDDIE SETSER and TROY SEALS

67

Verse 2:
She reached down and picked the gun up
That lay smokin' in his hand.
She said, "Father, please forgive me;
I can't make it without my man."
And she knew the gun was empty,
And she knew she couldn't win,
But her final prayer was answered
When the rifles fired again. *(To Chorus:)*

WILL YOU REMEMBER MINE

Words and Music by
WILLIE NELSON

Slowly, with expression

70

NO REASON TO QUIT

Words and Music by
DEAN HOLLOWAY

SPANISH EYES

Words by
CHARLES SINGLETON and EDDIE SNYDER

Music by
BERT KAEMPFERT

WHISKEY RIVER

By
JOHNNY BUSH

Whis-key Riv-er take my mind; don't let her

mem-'ry tor-ture me. Whis-key Riv-er don't run

dry. You're all I've got, take care of

me. Whis-key

CHANGING SKIES

Words and Music by
WILLIE NELSON

Slowly ♩ = 80

1. There's a bird ... in the sky
2. 4. *(See additional lyrics)*
3. *(Instrumental Solo ad lib.)*

fly - in' high, _____ fly - in'

high _____ to a place

Verse 2:
There are clouds in the sky;
Clouds of fear and despair.
But love like ours never dies.
Changing skies, changing skies.

Verse 4:
Little bird, have you heard
Freedom lies, freedom lies?
But love like ours never dies.
Changing skies, changing skies.

It's Not Supposed To Be That Way

Words and Music by
WILLIE NELSON

CROSSING THE BORDER

Words and Music by
KRIS KRISTOFFERSON

Slow but deliberate

STAY ALL NIGHT (STAY A LITTLE LONGER)

Words and Music by
TOMMY DUNCAN

er.

Coda

G7

(Play 12 times)
D.S. al 5th ending

2. Now you ought to see my blue-eyed Sally;
Lives way down on Shinbone Alley,
And the number on the gate
And the number on the door,
Next house over is a grocery store.

(To Chorus:)

3. *Instrumental*

4. *Instrumental*

5. Take your mama, stand her on the head.
If she don't like this, can you feed her cornbread?
Gals around big creek about half drawn;
Jump on a man like a dog on a bone.

(To Chorus:)

YESTERDAY'S WINE

Words and Music by
WILLIE NELSON

3. You give the appearance of one widely travelled;.
   I'll bet you've seen things in your time;
   So sit down beside me and tell me your story,
   If you think you'll like yesterday's wine.

I AM THE FOREST

Words and Music by
WILLIE NELSON

FORGIVING YOU WAS EASY

Words and Music by
WILLIE NELSON

Verse 2:
The bitter fruit of anger growin' from the seeds of jealousy;
Oh, what a heartache, but I forgive the things you said to me.
'Cause I believe forgiving is the only way that I'll find peace of mind.
And forgiving you is easy, but forgetting seems to take the longest time.

Verse 3:
The years have passed so quickly, as once again fate steals a young man's dreams
Of all the golden years and growing old together, you and me.
You ask me to forgive you, you said there was another on your mind.
And forgiving you is easy, but forgetting seems to take the longest time.
Forgiving you is easy, but forgetting seems to take the longest time.

ANGEL FLYING TOO CLOSE TO THE GROUND

Words and Music by
WILLIE NELSON

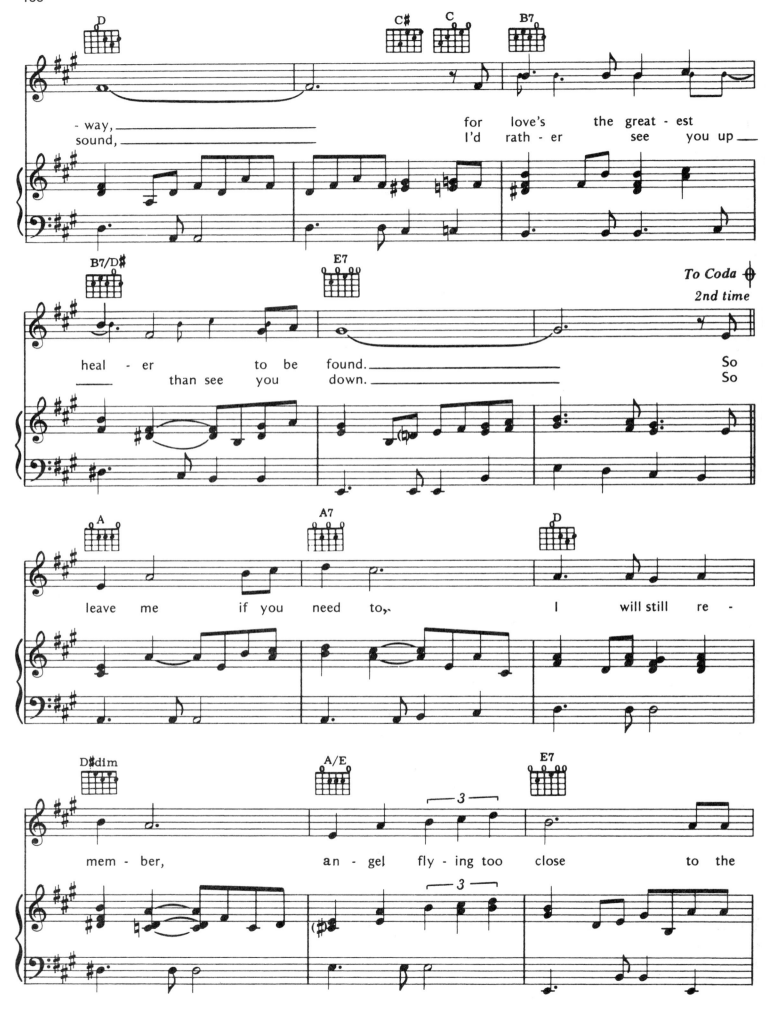

IF YOU CAN TOUCH HER AT ALL

Words and Music by
LEE CLAYTON

Moderate Waltz tempo

1. Fun - ny   a wom - an   can come on   so wild and free,
2. One night   of love   don't make up   for six nights a - lone,
3. Right   or wrong   a wom - an   can own an - y man,

Yet in - sist I don't
I'd rath - er have
She can take him in -

watch her un - dress   or watch her watch   me.
one   than none   'cause I'm flesh and   bone.
side her and   hold   his soul   in her   hand.

I'D HAVE TO BE CRAZY

Words and Music by
STEVE FROMHOLZ

I'd have to be cra-zy to stop all my sing-in' and nev-er play mus-ic a-gain.

You'd call me a fool if I grabbed up a top hat and

112

2. Now I know I've done weird things
   Told people I heard things
   When silence was all that abound
   Been days when it pleased me
   To be on my knees following ants as they crawled 'cross the ground.
   I been insane on a train
   But I'm still me again
   The place where I hold you is true.
   I know I'm all-right
   'Cause I'd have to be crazy to fall out of love with you.

BRIDGE

3. I sure would be dingy
   To live in an envelope
   Just a-waitin' alone for a stamp
   You'd say I was loco
   If I rubbed for a genie while burning my hand on the lamp.
   I may not be normal
   But nobody is.
   I'd like to say 'fore I'm through
   I'd have to be crazy plumb out of my mind
   To fall out of love with you.
   I'd have to be crazy
   Plumb out of my mind to fall out of love with you.

I'M A MEMORY

Words and Music by
WILLIE NELSON

mind. _____
long. _____

Close your eyes; I'm a

mem-'ry. _____ I'm a mem-'ry. _____

Repeat and fade

3. I'm a dream that comes with the night;
   I'm a face that fades with the light;
   I'm a tear that falls out of sight;
   Close your eyes, I'm a memory.

BLACK ROSE

Words and Music by
BILLY JOE SHAVER

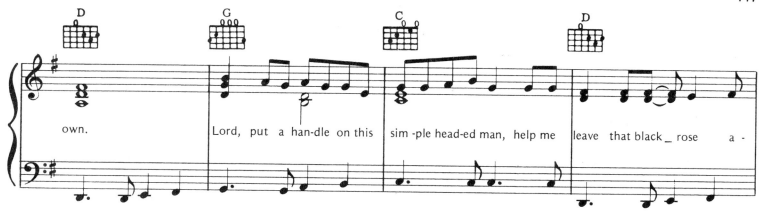

own.　　Lord, put a han-dle on this　　sim-ple head-ed man, help me　　leave that black _ rose　　a-

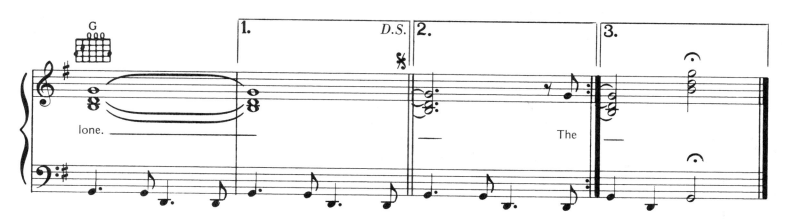

lone. _____　　　1.　　　　　D.S. 2.　　　　　The　　　3.

Verse 2:
The first time I felt lightning
I was standin' in the drizzlin' rain
With a tremblin' hand and a bottle of gin
And a rose of a different name. (To Chorus:)

Verse 3:
When the devil made that woman,
Lord, he threw the pattern away.
She were built for speed with the tools you need
To make a new fool everyday.

Verse 4:
Way down deep and dirty,
On the darkest side of shame
You'll find this cane raisin' man doin' it again
With a rose of a different name. (To Chorus:)

TWILIGHT TIME

Words by
BUCK RAM

Music by
MORTY NEVINS and AL NEVINS

PANCHO AND LEFTY

By
TOWNES VAN ZANDT

1. Liv - ing on the road, _____ my friend, _____
2. 3. 4. (See additional lyrics)

123

D.S.(3rd Verse)
D.SS.(Instr.)
D.S.(4th Verse)
D.SS. al Coda

out of kind-ness I __ sup-pose.

pose.

Verse 2:
Pancho was a bandit boy,
His horse was fast as polished steel.
He wore his gun outside his pants,
For all the honest world to feel.
Well, Pancho met his match, you know,
On the deserts down in Mexico.
Nobody heard his dying word,
Ah, but that's the way it goes.

Verse 3:
Lefty, he can't sing the blues,
All night long like he used to.
The dust that Pancho bit down south,
Ended up in Lefty's mouth.
The day they laid poor Pancho low,
Lefty split for Ohio.
Where he got the bread to go,
There ain't nobody know.

Verse 4:
The poets tell how Pancho felt,
And Lefty's living in a cheap hotel;
The desert's quiet, and Cleveland's cold,
And so the story ends we're told.
Pancho needs your prayers, it's true,
And save a few for Lefty, too.
He only did what he had to do,
And now, he's growing old.

WHY DO I HAVE TO CHOOSE

Words and Music by
WILLIE NELSON

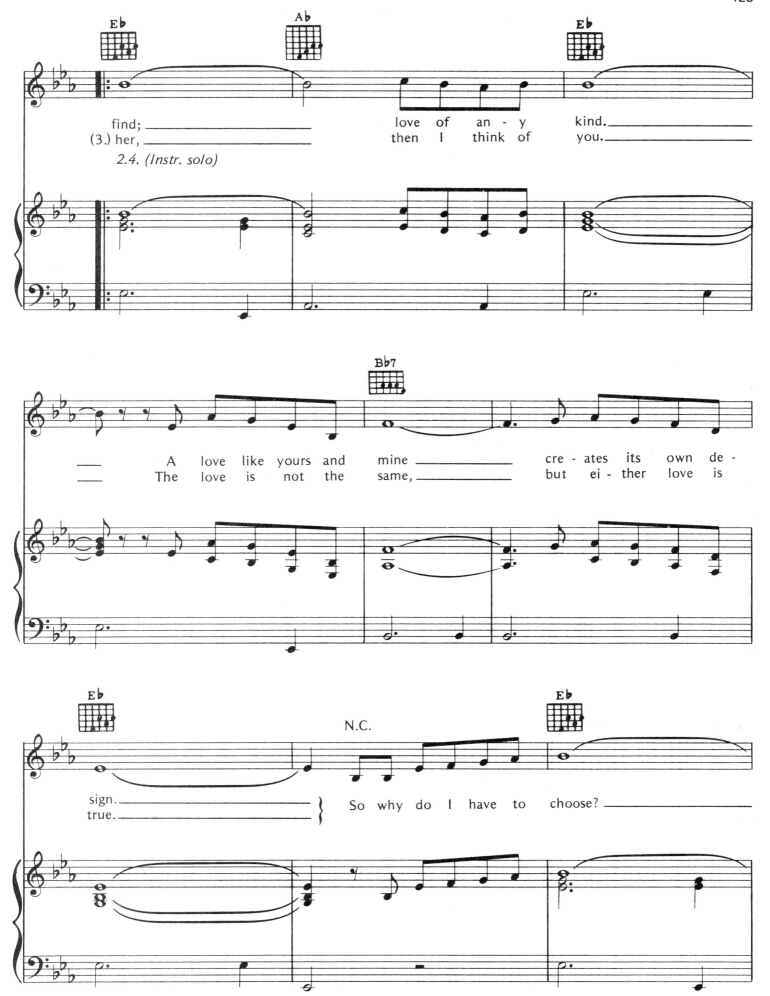

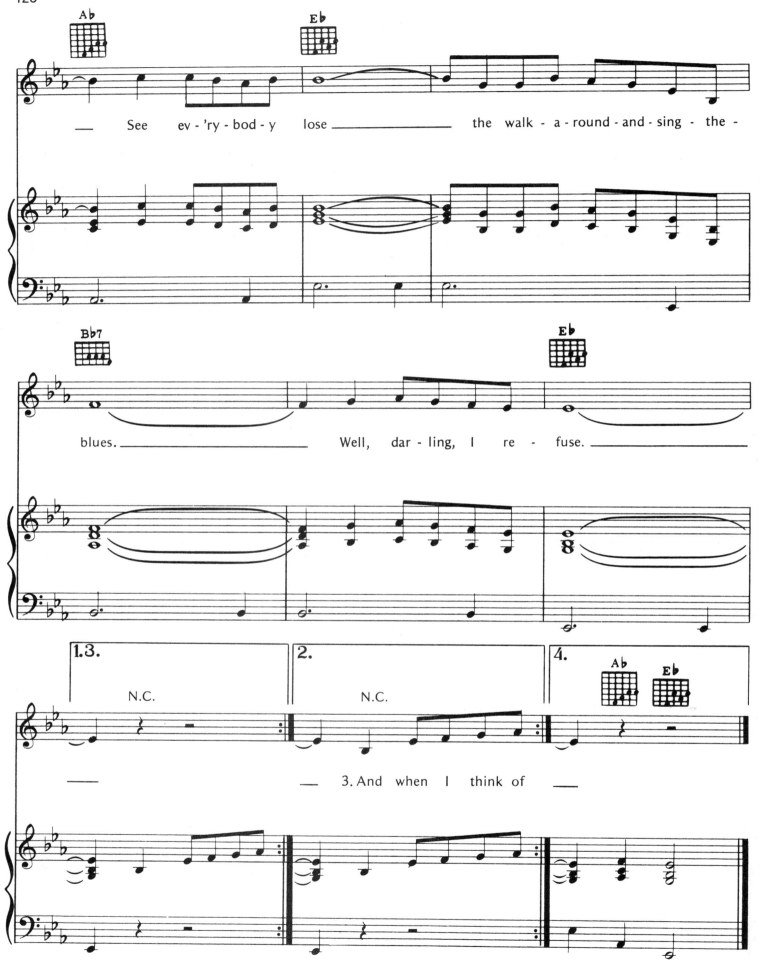

Heartbreak Hotel

Words and Music by
MAE BOREN AXTON,
TOMMY DURDEN and ELVIS PRESLEY

down at the end of Lone - ly Street, that Heart - break Ho-
bro - ken heart - ed lov - ers to cry a - way their

tel, and I get so lone - ly, ba - by,
gloom, and I get so lone - ly, ba - by,

I get so lone - ly ba - by, I get so lone-
I get so lone - ly ba - by, I get so lone-

Verses 3 & 4:
Instrumental solo

Verse 5:
Well, the bellhop's tears keep flowing,
The desk clerk's dressed in black,
They've been so long on Lonely Street
They'll never, never, never get back.
I've been so lonely, baby, I get so lonely baby,
I get so lonely I could die.

Verse 6:
So, if your baby leaves you,
You got a tale to tell,
Just take a walk down Lonely Street,
To Heartbreak Hotel.
I get so lonely, baby, I get so lonely, baby,
I get so lonely I could die.

Verse 7:
Instrumental solo

IF YOU'VE GOT THE MONEY, I'VE GOT THE TIME

By
LEFTY FRIZZELL and JIM BECK

I've got the time.____

3. We'll go honky tonkin';
   Make ev'ry spot in town.
   We'll go to the park where it's dark
   And we won't fool around.
   If you run short of money,
   I'll run short of time.
   You got no more money, honey,
   I've no more time.
   If you've got the money, honey,
   I've got the time.
   We'll go honky tonkin'
   And we'll have a time.
   Bring along your Cadillac;
   Leave my old wreck behind.
   If you've got the money, honey,
   I've got the time.

BLOODY MARY MORNING

Words and Music by
WILLIE NELSON

It's a Blood-y Ma-ry morn-ing, ba-by left me with-out

warn-ing some time in the night.

(Guitar fill)

So I'm fly-ing down to Hous-ton, with for-get-ting her the

135

MAMMAS DON'T LET YOUR BABIES GROW UP TO BE COWBOYS

Moderate ♩ = 63

Words and Music by
ED BRUCE and PATSY BRUCE

Cow-boys ain't eas-y to love and they're hard-er to hold.
Cow-boys like smok-y old pool rooms and clear moun-tain morn-ings,

They'd rath-er give you a
lit-tle warm pup-pies and

song than dia-monds or gold.
chil-dren and girls of the night.

Lone Star belt buck-les___ and old fad-ed Le-vis and each night be-
Them that don't know him___ won't like him and them that do some-times won't

gins___ a new day. If you don't un-der-stand him and
know how to take him. He ain't wrong he's just dif-f'rent but his

he don't die___ young he'll prob-'ly just ride___ a - way.⎱
pride won't___ let him do things to make you think___ he's right.⎰

cresc.

141

WITHOUT A SONG

Words by
WILLIAM ROSE and EDWARD ELISCU

Music by
VINCENT YOUMANS

MOON RIVER

Words and Music by
JOHNNY MERCER

Music by
HENRY MANCINI

TO EACH HIS OWN

By
JAY LIVINGSTON and RAY EVANS

A Good Hearted Woman

Words and Music by
WILLIE NELSON and WAYLON JENNINGS

1.) A long time for - got - ten, are dreams that just
2.) He likes the night life, are the bright lights just and

fell by the way.
good - tim - in' friends.

And the good life he prom - ised ain't what she's
When the par - ty's all ov - er she'll wel - come

had   and all   the   good times   to ___ come.
she   loves   her   good - tim - in' ___ man.

Chorus:

She's   a   good - heart - ed   wo - man ___ in   love   with   a

good - tim - in'   man.   She

loves   him   in   spite   of   his   ways   that   she   don't   un - der - stand.

All Of Me

Words and Music by
GERALD MARKS and SEYMOUR SIMONS

I STILL CAN'T BELIEVE YOU'RE GONE

Words and Music by
WILLIE NELSON

CRAZY

Words and Music by
WILLIE NELSON

SEPTEMBER SONG

Words by
MAXWELL ANDERSON

Music by
KURT WEILL

coup-le of whirls, While I plied her with tears in lieu of pearls And as
goods they bring, They have lit-tle to of-fer but the songs they sing And a

time came a-round she came my way, As time came a-round she came.
plen-ti-ful waste of time of day, A plen-ti-ful waste of time.

Refrain *(with expression)*

Oh, it's a long, long while From May to De - cem - ber,—

But the days grow short_____ When you reach Sep-

Railroad Lady

Words and Music by
JIMMY BUFFETT and JEFF WALKER

She's a Rail - road La - dy just a lit - tle bit
sha - dy spend - ing her days on the trains.

She's a se - mi good - look - er but the fast rails they
Once a Pull - man car trav - el - ler, now the switch - man won't

She
Now that the rail - packs has taken the best
hocked 'em for cold cash left town on the

tracks, _____ she's try - in', just try - in' to get home a -
Wa - bash, ne -ver think - ing, nev - er think - ing of home way back

to Coda ⊕ 1. C7 She's a 2. C D.S. %: al ⊕ Coda 3. But the To Chorus al fine She's a
gain.
then.

Coda

168

Verse 3   But the rails are now rusty; The dining car's dusty; The gold-plated watches have
taken their toll; The railroads are dying; And the lady, she's crying; On a bus to
Kentucky and home that's her goal. (Repeat Cho.)

WE HAD IT ALL

By
DONNIE FRITTS and TROY SEALS

OLD FRIENDS

Words and Music by
ROGER MILLER

Slowly

1. Old friends pitch-in' pen-nies in the park, play-in'

2. Old   *Instrumental Solo*

Repeat ad lib. and fade

HARBOR LIGHTS

Slowly (with expression)

Words and Music by
JIMMY KENNEDY and HUGH WILLIAMS

One eve-ning long a-go, a big ship was leav-ing, One eve-ning long a-go, two lov-ers were griev-ing, A crim-son sun went down, the lights be-gan to glow.

DEVIL IN A SLEEPING BAG

Words and Music by
WILLIE NELSON

We were head-ed home to Aus-tin; caught pneu-mon-ia on the
back from New York Cit-y; Kris and Rit-a done it

road, _____ tak-ing it home to Con-nie and the
all, _____ raw per-fec-tion there for all the worlds to

road is such a drag. _____ If we can

make it home by Fri-day, we can brag." _____ And the

to Coda ⊕

dev - il shiv - ered in his sleep-in' bag. _____ Well, I just got

2.   D.S. al Coda ⊕

bag. _____ And the

Coda

bag. _____

HEALING HANDS OF TIME

Words and Music by
WILLIE NELSON

G
sleep a - gain, those heal - ing hands of time. So al -
G7
C
read - y I've reached moun - tain peaks, and I've just be - gun to
G
D7
climb; I'll get ov - er you by cling - ing to those heal - ing hands of
1.
G
C
C
D
time. They're
2.
C
G
D7
G
Fine
time.

TO ALL THE GIRLS I'VE LOVED BEFORE

Lyrics by
HAL DAVID

Music by
ALBERT HAMMOND

NIGHT LIFE

Words and Music by
WILLIE NELSON,
WALT BREELAND and PAUL BUSKIRK

ME AND PAUL

Words and Music by
WILLIE NELSON

takin' sev - 'ral read - ings, I'm sur - prised to find my
stay - in' in a mo - tel there and leave, just don't leave

D7

mind still fair - ly sound.
noth - in' in your clothes.

G

I guess Nash - ville was the rough - est, but I
And at the air - port in Mil - wauk - ee, they re -

know I said the same a - bout them all.
fused to let us board the plane at all.

We re - ceived our ed - u - ca - tion in the
They said we looked sus - pic - ious, but I be -

cit - ies of the na - tion, me and Paul.
lieve they liked to pick on me and Paul. (Repeat Verse 1)

1. 2. 3. 4.   5.   Repeat and fade

2. Al - most
3. It's been
4. On a
5. It's been

On a package show in Buffalo, with us and Kitty Wells and Charlie Pride;
The show was long and we're just sittin' there,
And we'd come to play and not just for the ride;
Well, we drank a lot of whiskey, so I don't know if we went on that night at all;
I don't think they even missed us;
I guess Buffalo ain't geared for me and Paul;
(Repeat Verse 1)

UP AGAINST THE WALL REDNECK

Words and Music by
RAY WYLIE HUBBARD

With a beat

He was born in Ok-la-ho-ma, and his wife's name is Bet-ty Lou Thel-ma Liz. And he's not re-spon-si-ble for what he's do-in',

THE CONVICT AND THE ROSE

Words and Music by
BETTY CHAPIN and ROBERT KING

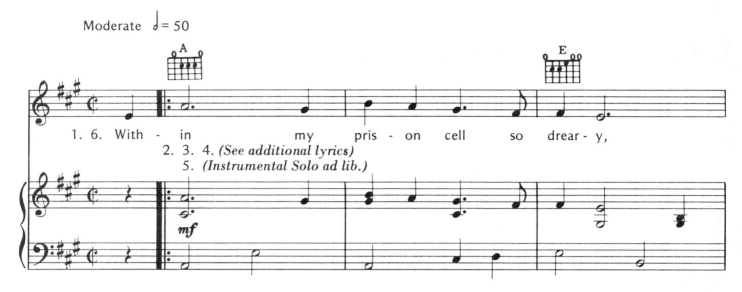

1. 6. With - in my pris - on cell so drear - y,
2. 3. 4. (See additional lyrics)
5. (Instrumental Solo ad lib.)

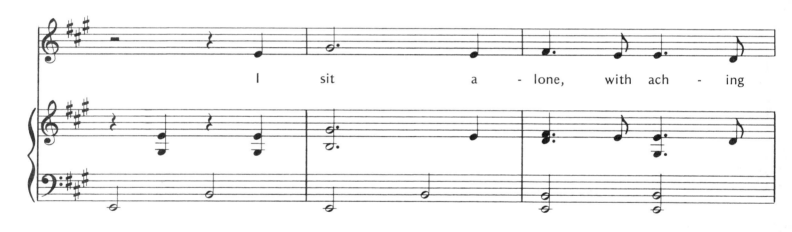

I sit a - lone, with ach - ing

heart.

I'm dream - ing

Verse 2:
The rose, she sent me as a token.
She sent it just to lighten my gloom.
And tell me that her heart was broken,
And cheer me before I meet my doom.

Verse 3:
The judge would not believe my story.
The jury said I'd have to pay.
And with the rose and all it's glory,
"Not guilty," was all that I could say.

Verse 4:
Goodbye sweetheart, for in the morning,
To meet my maker, I must go.
And when I die at daylight's dawning,
Against my heart they'll find this rose.

IT'S MY LAZY DAY

By
SMILEY BURNETTE

Moderate country shuffle ♩ = 120

1. Well, I might have gone __ fish - ing; __ I got to think-ing it
2. *(See additional lyrics)*

o - ver; the road to the riv - er, is a might-y long __ way. Oh, it must be the

204

Verse 2:
And never mind calling,
'Cause I aint coming.
Just get you on by me;
Stay out of my way.
A little deep thinking;
Drive me to drinking;
I'm taking it easy;
It's my lazy day.

Verse 3:
(same as verse 1.)

SUFFERING IN SILENCE

Words and Music by
WILLIE NELSON

Slow Waltz Tempo

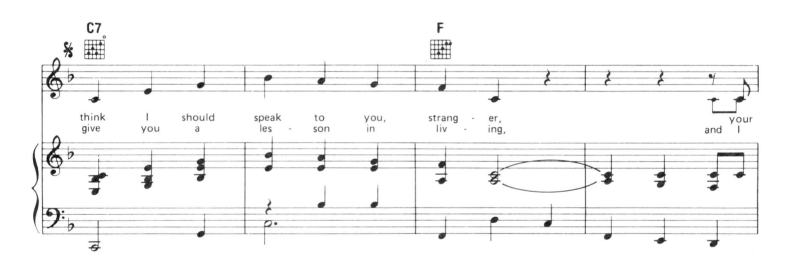

think I should speak to you, strang - er,
give you a les - son in liv - ing,
and I your

prob - lem is clear now to me.
hope it stays with you a - while.
You
You're the

MY HEROES HAVE ALWAYS BEEN COWBOYS

Words and Music by
SHARON VAUGHN

209

The Shelter Of Your Arms

Words and Music by
SHIRLEY COLLIE

THE WORDS DON'T FIT THE PICTURE

Words and Music by
WILLIE NELSON

Moderately Slow

If this is a game we play, and if this is a role I play, where are the words ____ I say to you?

UNCLOUDY DAY

Arrangement by
WILLIE NELSON

SPIRIT

Words and Music by
KENT M. ROBBINS and WILL ROBINSON

221

D.S. 𝄋

Repeat ad lib. and fade

Verse 2:
As the sunset led him homeward,
He saw clouds of smoke above the trees.
He cut his ponies loose and rode just like the wind.
He could smell the white man on the breeze.
To Bridge:

Verse 3:
White Eagle watched the fall of Custer,
Died a hundred times at Wounded Knee.
Walked with his homeless brothers down this Trail of Tears
On his path through history.
To Bridge:

LOOK WHAT THOUGHTS WILL DO

By
LEFTY FRIZZELL,
DUB DICKERSON and JIM BECK

just look what _____ love will _____

do. _____

2. And if, within your future years,
   Your new love should bring you tears,
   And you'll think of me, I'm sure,
   But those thoughts won't help you, dear.
   Once I thought I loved just you;
   And I thought you loved me, too,
   But today you say we're through.
   Now, just look what thoughts will do.

BLUE EYES CRYING IN THE RAIN

By
FRED ROSE

HALF A MAN

Words and Music by
WILLIE NELSON

Slow country waltz ♩ = 76

LITTLE OLD FASHIONED KARMA

Fast country ♩ = 104

Words and Music by
WILLIE NELSON

Georgia On My Mind

Words by
STUART GORRELL

Music by
HOAGY CARMICHAEL

HEAVEN AND HELL

Words and Music by
WILLIE NELSON

And some - times it's heav - en, and some - times it's

hell, and some - times I don't e - ven know.

1. 2. D. S. al Coda

Well,

know.

Coda

A DREAMER'S HOLIDAY

Words by
KIM GANNON

Music by
MABEL WAYNE

Moderately (with a lift)

Chorus:

Climb a-board a but-ter-fly and take off on the breeze Let your wor-ries flut-ter by and do the things you please In the land where dol-lar bills are

And So Will You, My Love

Words and Music by
WILLIE NELSON

BLACKJACK COUNTY CHAINS

Words and Music by
RED LANE

Moderately

1. *Instrumental Solo*
2. I was sit-tin' be-side the road ___ in Black-jack
3. 4. 5. *(See additional lyrics)*
6. 7. etc. *(Instrumental Solo)*

Coun-ty, not know-ing that the sher-iff paid a

boun-ty for men like me who

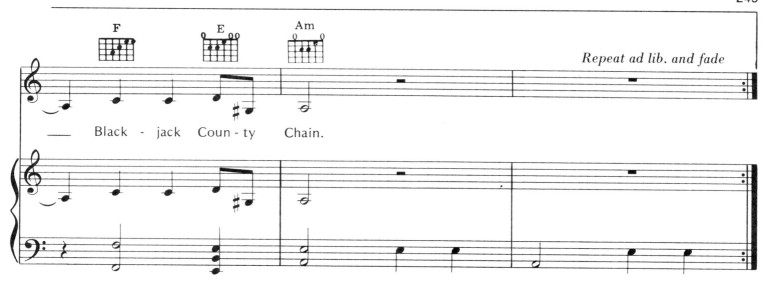

Black - jack Coun - ty Chain.

Repeat ad lib. and fade

Verse 3:

And all we had to eat was bread and water,

And each day we had to build that road a mile and a quarter;

And a black-snake whip would cut our backs when some poor fool complained.

But we couldn't fight back wearing 35 pounds of Blackjack County Chain.

Verse 4:

Then one night while the sheriff was a-sleeping,

We all gathered 'round him, slowly creeping;

And heaven help me to forget that night in the cold, cold rain,

When we beat him to death with the 35 pounds of Blackjack County Chain.

Verse 5:

Now the whip marks have all healed and I'm thankful

That there's nothing but a scar around my ankle;

But most of all I'm glad no man will be a slave again

To a black-snake whip and 35 pounds of Blackjack County Chain.

(Repeat last line)

Verse 6, 7: etc.

Instrumental

Help Me Make It Through The Night

Words and Music by
KRIS KRISTOFFERSON

WHY BABY WHY

Words and Music by
GEORGE JONES and DARRELL EDWARDS

Verse 2:
Well, now, I don't know, but I've heard say,
That every little dog's a-gonna have his day;
You better pay attention, don't you dare forget,
'Cause I'm just a little baby puppy yet.
I caught you honky tonkin' with my best friend;
The thing to do was leave you, but I should-a left then.
Now I'm too old to leave you but I still get sore,
When you come home a-feel-in' for the knob on the door.
(To Chorus:)